JENIFER R. FENNELL

Keep Living

A JOURNAL FOR HEALING THROUGH YOUR GRIEF

Keep Living
A Journal for Healing Through your Grief

Written by Jenifer R. Fennell

© 2020 J.R. Allen Consulting

J.R. Allen Conulting
Kansas City, KS
jrallenconsulting@outlook.com

Ordering Information:Quantity sales. Special discounts are available on quantity purchases by corporations, associations, and others. For details, contact the publisher at the email address above.

Orders by U.S. trade bookstores and wholesalers.

Paperback ISBN: 978-0-578-77545-6

Printed in the United States of America
10 9 8 7 6 5 4 3 2 1
First Edition

My dearest brother T, You will forever be engraved in my heart.

I loved you then, I love you now, and I will love you forever.

I am my brothers keeper.

I wake up and I cry every morning.
Another day here, on earth.
It's not the greatest feeling at first, I'll admit.
Because at night I dream of you...
And when I wake
I know you aren't here
to walk in the light With me.

I know that I'll have to put the weight of your loss down
For a minute.

So I can get out of my bed
So I can enjoy a nice walk.
Or sit with my mom to have coffee.

I know that I have to put the thought of you aside.

So that I can smile at the mailman
and tell him good morning.
Maybe his morning wasn't so good.

I've got to tuck you away,

So I can be on time for work
So that I can be inspired by something...

And at night,I close my eyes.
Where you'll meet me at the portal.

And my mind dances with the thoughts I've longed to
think,
All day.

-Asia Upton

Keep Living

Keep Living...Whoa! Those two words are huge.
Keep living is a big step. When people told me
that I have to keep living after my brother passed
away, I used to think how? How do I keep living
without the most important person in my life? How
do you want me do to that? Please tell me how?
As my days became longer and my nights became
shorter, I had to figure out life again, because I
had to be here for the people who are still living
life on this Earth, so here we are.

I know you are wondering how and why I named this
journal Keep Living; it is because those words are
true. In order to survive the pain and the loss of your
loved one, I learned personally that you absolutely
must keep living. We have to keep living for our
surviving loved ones. We have to keep living to
ensure that our children, our children's children, our
family, and our friends will have the opportunity to
keep living in the legacy of our lost loved one.

It's okay to cry silently, it's okay to scream at the top of your lungs, it's okay to be angry, trust me, I've been there. But a little voice in me starting saying, it's okay, you're okay. We don't know what the afterlife entails, but what I do know is that I want to see my brother again and when I do, I'm never letting him go. This journal is for me to keep living for him, and for my mom. Without the power of journaling, I would not have been able to keep living. By creating this journal, I wanted to give you the quotes that helped me along this grief journey and my hope is that you will also find the power of journaling as well. Journal when you are angry at the world, when you are sad, happy, feel guilty that you are still here, feeling loved, or just because, so that you can find peace during your grief, to find the strength and the words to just KEEP LIVING!

THE REALITY IS
THAT YOU WILL
GRIEVE FOREVER.
YOU WILL NOT
"GET OVER" THE
LOSS OF A LOVED
ONE; YOU WILL
LEARN TO LIVE
WITH IT. YOU
WILL HEAL AND
YOU WILL REBUILD
YOURSELF
AROUND THE LOSS
YOU HAVE
SUFFERED. YOU
WILL BE WHOLE
AGAIN BUT YOU
WILL NEVER BE
THE SAME. NOR
SHOULD YOU BE
THE SAME, NOR
WOULD YOU WANT
TO.

-Karen Civil

March 3   VA

Breathing Exercise

Left Shoulder numbness Rt outside lower Arm.
11.00 Vision Good.
Am Shifting my head can position of headache sometime
     Protien B4 bed
     Sharp Pain below Rg Rib Bone deep
     Pressure. moves across forehead Blind Eyes?

                Video Call

Called Hillcrest South for Records.

Emirecy Reosed for transpor on 5.21-21
   this was transport from SB Libaby Pequired
   By librieus/Ems
      lost of Connection   small nausea
      light h-oded   unable to Return hom-
      Balance   on own
           Sudden occurance.
   I ve had serval of These occurance during
   '21 while I have been Required not to work
   even partime

   I have 2 kinds of Mirgaine 1st has a warning
   either nausea or light senistive these I
   can control and I don't go to hosp.tal

   The 2nd Kind are the kind mention on 5-21-2
   no warnings, varied reaction - these I report

Injuries - I dont want to call them
Disabilitys bc that gives them power

from my neck stiffness in the morning
which disturbs my sleep often waking me

I dont have a headache when I wake It
comes when I start to raise

Sometimes sleeping with a brace will
prevent the stiffness but I dont like sleeping
with interference

Upon raising the headache slowly Appears
usually Right temple, Back of head low
or across forehead and Eyes

the numbness in shoulder cap usually tak

4hours the numbness is in the shoulder
cap and the ~~artid~~ ulna and Radius

hands mostly thumbs and pointer fingres

---

thoracic area onthe left near spinal and
at bottom of shoulder blade feels Deep
mostly gone after change in 2013
acts up Rarely now and Doesnt feel as
deep Persist Ache? Right side 4" down From
Neck (2) these acting up usually are proceed by
Breast pain

upper lambor (Belt waist) level feels like poor stacking affects Bending + Bowel Control

lower to Tail Bone - frail, fragile, wide spread used to be always now wide the chiropatic lift the pain is less and with the Brace at work as a Remind to not overdue or lift is allowing me to Return to work at least 2 days a week I'm working on Building to 3 consecitive day

Before 2 days Running was Impossible and I usually had to sleep 8+ hours with not relief

My Indurance is poor!

With the Brace the Reaction is from hip Joins + tail bone sharp electric pain of short Burst tightness in Back of legs and heel pain mostly Right side sometime the Akilles Muscle

I've started (power walking) to Improve the glute muscles   using the full Range
                                            of muscle

Present Distance
1 mile out + Back
Caseys + Brarms

Word goal - 3 day/12 hours. - 36 hrs.

SOMETIMES WE DON'T WANT TO HEAL BECAUSE THE PAIN IS THE LAST LINK TO WHAT WE'VE LOST

-JM Storm

DEATH LEAVES A HEARTACHE NO ONE CAN HEAL, LOVE LEAVES A MEMORY NO ONE CAN STEAL

-Author Unknown

THE LORD HEARS HIS PEOPLE WHEN THEY CALL TO HIM FOR HELP. HE RESCUES THOSE WHOSE SPIRITS ARE CRUSHED

Psalm 34:17-18

IT'S NOT ABOUT GETTING OVER IT, ITS ABOUT LEARNING TO LIVE WITH YOUR NEW NORMAL, FINDING COMFORT IN THE CONSTANT PAIN OF LOSS

-discovering Danielle Simpson

YOU DON'T KNOW WHAT
STRENGTH AND
PERSEVERANCE IS UNTIL
YOU LOSE SOMEONE YOU
LOVE

-Aurthor Unknown

MAY YOUR HEART FIND PEACE DURING YOUR HEALING PROCESS.

-Jenifer Fennell

DON'T ALLOW OTHERS TO RUSH YOU THROUGH YOUR GRIEF, YOU HAVE A LIFETIME TO HEAL AND IT'S A LIFELONG JOURNEY AT YOUR OWN SPEED

-Aurthor Unknown

ONE DAY YOU WILL
TELL YOUR STORY OF
HOW YOU OVERCAME
WHAT YOU WENT
THROUGH AND IT WILL
BE SOMEONE ELSE'S
SURVIVAL GUIDE

-Aurthor Unknown

I WILL TURN
THEIR MOURNING
INTO GLADNESS,
I WILL GIVE
THEM COMFORT
AND JOY
INSTEAD OF
SORROW

-Jeremiah 31:13

THIS IS NOT THE
LIFE YOU
PICTURED BUT
HERE YOU ARE.
YOU CAN STILL
MAKE SOMETHING
BEAUTIFUL.GRIEVE
,BREATHE, BEGIN
AGAIN!

-DR. THEMA

APPRECIATE LIFE TODAY MORE THAN EVER, MORE THAN YOU DID YESTERDAY, AND TOMORROW, APPRECIATE LIFE MORE TOMORROW THAN YOU DO TODAY BECAUSE LIFE ISN'T PROMISED

-Ellen Degeneres

THEY EXISTED.
THEY EXISTED.
WE CAN BE.
BE AND BE BETTER.
FOR THEY EXISTED

-Maya Angelou

WE NEED TO GRIEVE
THE ONES WE HAVE
LOVED AND LOST IN
THIS LIFETIME — NOT
TO SUSTAIN OUR
CONNECTION TO
SUFFERING, BUT TO
SUSTAIN OUR
CONNECTION TO
LOVE.

-JW

SMILE THOUGH
YOUR HEART IS
ACHING, SMILE
EVEN THOUGH IT'S
BREAKING. WHEN
THERE ARE CLOUDS
IN THE SKY, YOU'LL
GET BY.

IF YOU SMILE
THROUGH YOUR
FEAR AND SORROW,
SMILE AND MAYBE
TOMORROW, YOU'LL
SEE THE SUN COME
SHINING THROUGH
FOR YOU

-Nat King Cole